MW01610257

listen
2 the future

listen 2 the future

stewart sealy

LISTEN 2 THE FUTURE
copyright © 2021 by stewart sealy
all rights reserved
no part of this book may be used or reproduced in any manner
whatsoever without written permission except in the case of
brief quotations embodied in critical articles and reviews
for more information, email author

cover created by leta taylor (www.spacesofarcadia.com)

email iamstewartsealy@gmail.com
instagram @iamstewartsealy

listen
2 the future

**stewart
sealy**

preface

what would you do if i told you that the future has planned a
visit to our present experiences?
with warnings in the form of poetic visions

like a mirror reflecting back to us our own fate of a world in
perilous times
if we do not amend our ways

what would you do if you knew that the future will not be
written unless you write it?

do you really want to fight the monsters of famine
plagues
and wars?

would it be wise to open pandora's box
or to eat the forbidden fruit?

the seeds that we plant today will be the shade the next
generation will sit under
or the fires that they will have to put out

if we don't give heed to the visitation by the future
i fear that it will leave us
and fast forward to its awaited time
and we shall have the history we make in the present

other futures did visit in times past
but were killed when we saw its reflection

Stewart Sealy

listen 2 the future

the bird dies to let another fly
        the road ends to begin again
                the ink dries so the paper won't cry

the moon drops down to let the sun have a day
and love sacrifices to love again
after the pain

dedication

this book is dedicated to great minds that think alike
to those that see the urgency of the times
and to
all my family members that celebrate my life

i set poetic visions before you
that if we look and not see
we will hear the wings of the future loud and clear
this book leads us to the mirror of our ways
and may we pray for better days
as we make a change

contents

contents

contents

contents

are
_____

listen 2 the future

don't go to earth

the road will be dusty
the nails will be rusty

you will wear odd-looking clothes
you will be misunderstood
and humans will stare at you strangely
and force strong wine upon your lips

many will gamble for your cloak
they will hate your face for being peaceful

the sky will blacken
and you will feel forsaken
yet
the poor will be thankful
when you make them rich in faith
and bankrupt the rich in their souls

the powers that be will give you a painful crown

they will sing as the hammer puts nails in your hands and feet
and you feel it in your soul

don't go to earth
your visit will be short
dark angels will laugh in glee behind the scenes
but they will bend the knee

you felt compelled to leave heaven at the human cries
and you put on your human disguise

now you hang on a wooden tree
to sit one day with humanity

now free

the race

i hope you're serious
you're in the human race

no real privilege
death is a label all shall wear
run to win the real prize
eternal life

stop the black and white games
the death angel cares for no names

run smart before you start
embrace a brother

one blood speaks louder

the death angel checks your number of days
waiting to put you in his chains

stop the black and white games

the real enemy is the one you don't see in the race

fake love

fake love chips like paint
it falls to the ground in flakes

it's not snow falling
it's love melting

true love never fails

the dark is coming

stars will start falling
the sun will flick the switch to let the night begin

confusion will set in
the days of noah will sign in for a long shift

people running with no clue
forgetting the voice of prophets they once slew

truth they left behind
for ads that paint a good lie

buying and selling
your just a number
but that's why we care about you

the dark is coming
the grave is asking for more
but the good news is that heaven is asking for you too

i put my finger in my ears
i don't want to hear what i already know
the world is changing
and so are you
reminds me of autumn
and i fear winter is coming

your hands are becoming unsteady
and so are your feelings
and it feels so cold now in my bones

i remember when you dropped off your thoughts on my
doorstep
and i made a paper plane with it

the world is changing
and so are you
and it is winter now

watch out for falling bricks

i worry that hate stands as tall as buildings
and it is protected by egos well hidden

some have degrees hanging on their walls for getting a 100%
for prejudging

well done

killer whales help their own
i don't see them hating
and they travel in a crew

i worry about human intelligence
and i see hate standing so tall
ready to fall

watch out for falling egos
they hit as hard as bricks

face 2 face

every human being has already been
only now it's an earthly experience
call it living in the wind

feel it on your face
we are one human race

one day i won't see you anymore
every human being has already been

dust for clothes
so you can see me temporarily

really?
are you white and am i black?
we gonna play it like that?

blood is red
ask the dead

every human being has already been

the power of your greatness

don't live another day without your greatness being
extraordinary
you were wired for success
lies will short-circuit

don't let your greatness and you have a funeral
or you will live in regret

powerlessness is a mind-set
take leadership over negativity

this is not a play on words
this is a battle and only one will win
success or regrets?

be your own hero

act the part
you're on stage for the rest of your life

you're the hero in every chapter
and the villains will surround you

do what you would do to rescue a friend
save yourself
you need a hero

the monsters under the bed are already dead
you slayed them all last night in your dreams
a hero in your sleep

a new chapter with good news
the wicked witch is dead

that hero was always in you

the drifter

your mind needs a reset to stop thinking that you have lost and
not won

every drifting thought wants to settle in to get off the street
and out of the cold for some heat

stop giving yourself intelligent reasons for why you can't be a
genius

thoughts have a personality like a stamp stuck on a letter
the moment you open it it's now your story

the drifter is the opposite of positive thoughts
it goes by another name other than drifter
negativity it whispers

second start

when your heart wears a scar
sing again

push through to the stars and through the curtains of your
fears
let the light shine on your soul once again

pick up that pen and write again

when everyone stops believing in you
get your second wind
and god will help you to win

can i have this dance

with the last glance my eyes asked for this dance

i noticed that you were alone
destiny meeting us on the dance floor

my final hope
to share what only the stars can see
two people looking for a second chance to get love right
and start their new destiny

broken vows
lost rings

can i have this dance?

i noticed that you were alone tonight

traffic jam

confusion
two rings
both asking for you

but you can only give one hand

both glitter
but one is not gold
the other is silver

one to the left
the other to the right

loving both is breaking all the rules
traffic jam

you will remember one and forget the other

a traffic jam

emotional crash

incognito

don't think you know me
i am not superficial

undercover on the cross

i look human
but i am god
incognito

i had grief on my face but peace in my heart

i feed the poor and save the lost
incognito

you can miss me on your journey

first impressions do not impress heaven
a king with no crown does

if you will truly be great
you will wash earthly feet
incognito

thorns on the rose

blood on my hand
the rose is red
can't you tell?

beauty is fading
and what i lost in one day

a mystery
the book with no name
yet i pick another
hoping to give it to you
my hand will heal

the rose is still red
this is for you

don't bend my hope

the city feels alive
i see you across the street

i drop my fear and i dash to get your number
then i see him give you flowers

don't bend my hope
it might break

i know you did not make a mistake
we were meant to meet on this street
and destiny won't disappoint me

don't bend my hope
it might break

plastic island

plastic ocean
big fish choking
we are not learning the lessons

mankind is drifting
the planet is hurting

i saw lions walking in the streets
ancient prophecies

the time will come when the dead will speak again

forests burning
smoke in the clouds
we're not seeing

birds crashing into glass buildings

people with no clue text messaging

bank machines with their own identity telling you what to do

the house police can now open or lock your door with a cell phone

final warning

can you see it

bones making noise in tired bodies
retirement masquerading as final bliss

a pale horse is running called death
soldiers hit by smart bullets
fighting starts in the mind because of the lies we heard in
school

a red horse is running called war
a desperate cry for organic foods
intelligent chemicals
genetic mutes in the garden

a black horse is running called famine
robots have faces
and real people now are faceless

a white horse is running called conquer
a one-world system to ponder

break the spell

the clock is striking twelve
the internet is casting a spell

we are forgetting true friends
spies hiding in digital books

break the spell

rats fighting for food and the poor are sleeping on cold floors

wake up
this is not a fantasy

cyber bombs eliminating your intellectual property
in a dehumanized economy

break the spell

life on the outside

don't kid yourself
life on the outside is another prison cell

the joneses can't keep up

wallets full of credit cards are maxed out to stressful limits

we play our cards in a gambling game in a cashless society

life on the outside is no cup of tea
nine to five is a deep philosophy

the prison you will never see

public news

government for dummies
oppressive policies
nine to five times ten

robots sign paychecks
not there to make a friend

banks
merciless if you are not a shareholder
the money only gets colder

ropes around the neck
strangled with debt

whales crying from oceans for help
haunting the night
trees asking for water in the firefight

the mars projects
a billion dollars
and the poor live in cardboard boxes

public news

pray

we are on the big screen
faces screaming

time to kneel and send a prayer for world peace

stay on your knees until the world heals
give the poor what they need
respect and a meal

mixed minds create lies
saying *world peace* while they build weapons of war

birds clutter the sky
lost in their direction
trusting mankind
with a so-called intelligent mind

pray that we don't lose our way
someone has to pave the way

pray

till we all have faces

what does love look like breaking like glass from a hammer shattered?

i fear sharks are on land
the ocean has dried up
and problems have started for man

we can turn it around like a moving cloud

till we all have faces
mortals will keep decaying
the hour is coming

when a seed is no longer unseen
but will turn into you and me
immortal beings

kingdoms will crumble
and strangers with crowns will build pearl cities for god to
dwell

till we all have faces
this is not the human race

who is listening to the voice crying in the wilderness?

till we all have faces

you can't take it with you

i will one day leave my house empty
it is made of clay
i rent it for an earthly stay
my material things will forget my name

birds will fly by my grave
it is okay
i am not home

the things that we don't see
never go away
faith
hope
and love
the greatest of these is love

don't build your life on sand
the sea will wash it all away
we are only clay

you can't take it with you
anyway

the eclipse

the night is ominous
the future dresses up incognito and disappears
to moonwalk backward in time
to step out the front door to the present world of humanity
on urgent business
to warn the busy to listen 2 the future

reverse the present before it moves forward and makes the
history we will regret

world leaders still playing military games we wish we could
undo
human dna is chemically changed
now smartly human and smartly machine

dolphins having board meetings with men and women to stop
killing their dreams

listen 2 the future

the thought police imprison the free-thinking
your crime is deprogramming their manipulations and freeing
the children to listen 2 the future

the religious and the atheists capture the originator of free-
thinking and nail him to a tree

an eclipse wears a black veil
mourning the dead

human hands write in blood
guilty for theft and illegally entering through the door without
an invitation

a new day breaks the morning

the price was paid and history was changed into the present day

listen 2 the future

unfinished business

nations in jeopardy
this is not a tv show
it is life and death for liberty

stolen continents done very efficiently with a pen
treaties written with no rules
using invisible ink

books locked up with the truth
the keys given to mice and men
with no common sense

unfinished business must be settled in the books
until stolen continents are out of the red

books

books sitting
left behind minds
collecting dust

faces that gravity wore down
pulling them like clay in kids hands
with no care in the world

cloning the answer to youthfulness
men and women desperate for immortality

killing the red trees
the oxygen we need to breathe
science cannot stop what is real
the death of you and me

lots of degrees won't give us an extension on life
we all will rely on government pensions

we can think forward to do something with it
but we can't think in the past and do anything about it

one book opens and another one closes
books sitting
aging

where do the children play

minefields
the only playground children play in
hopscotch and another one goes missing

plastic soldiers in little boys hands turn to machine guns
running neighborhoods

where do the children play?
back alleys with broken televisions and rats eating kfc

it's the business of downsizing humanity
it doesn't matter where the children play
hopscotch
and another one goes missing

rebellion on oppression

the pharaohs mastered the system of oppression
we mastered the rebellion

with straw on our backs
we planned our attacks
peace is an invisible sword staying calm in the storm

heaven ordered miracles that change a pharaoh's mind
we were his automation
but also
prisoners at war

the new future with a pharaoh's agenda
robots that don't feel
lining us up for the count
dna business for cyborg enhancement

the world is harvesting organs for profit
and hiding in the shadows is the rebellion

logical citizens
deprogramming ai systems
the machines act like humans
they can read our thoughts

run to the hills before they inject you with agreement pills
keep the rebellion strong
before our humanity is gone

where is she now

the apple is missing and i am lost in the garden
the tree of knowledge lied to us and took my woman from me

the snake turned out to be a dragon
we were warned that all that glitters is not gold

she is missing
lost among the trees
where is she now?
i see her shadow running from aging

my bones keep asking
what is happening?
and why are we so brittle?

my only answer is that we changed our future from
peace to pain

where is she now?

everything is missing

stolen

stolen dances given another name
bleeding rubber trees
white sticky blood turned into wheels for overseas powers

breaking backs with overload from free labor
or call it slavery

missing hands for low quotas tired of blood loss
the rubber trees scream at robbers for rape unseen

congo treasures disappear overseas
children without mothers or fathers

tall ships with steel whips fight the wind to collect hiding
bodies

birds with one eye
too painful to look at the undeveloping of africa

one day the congo will sail to floating wealth
overseas to take from cities under a higher-order
stolen
give it back

policing the world

control thoughts and you rule their habits

ticket their imaginations before dreams destroy our monopoly

let fear out of the cage and society will agree to being enslaved

teach inferiority and policing the world will be easy

lockdown

history writes more details with a determined hand
for it sits up at night with many stories to write

reports suddenly rolled in like fast-flying information drones

voices stressed
the world is under a viral attack
a pandemic

state of emergency takes effect
cities in one day panic as the numbers of deaths climb
and the living cry

conspiracy theories fly around
no time to read them
we are on lockdown
jobs are lost
some never to be found

the economies feel the jeopardy
panic shoppers start hoarding
survival of the fittest is in play

humor is a sign of fear
hospital front-line soldiers fight against this viral war
many hands make light work

the lock-down starts playing mind games as the quarantine
makes outside a temptation

stay off the streets
the cities a ghost-town
some bodies are walking around with masked faces
counting the days

we lost some battles
we saw some come back to life
we will win this war

the world has one flag
it is called *one humanity*

human resource

the underground city
a network of sophisticated condos and commerce
the upper world is toxic for mankind

trees and plants
genetically altered
now needing human protein to survive

the sunshine day laws got approved
read between the lines

date of birth gives access to sunshine and upper earth
once a year

only the robots are allowed to live above ground
to manage the underground world

children write stories of automated utopia
the human and robot wars begin

spy city

the morning was quiet
you could hear a pin drop in cyberspace

a thin fog moves in like cigarette smoke
police drones are up at dawn
zipping by like bats using echolocation

robots dressed in three-piece suits and off to work
while humans watch comedy shows
the city listens and watches for law and order

politics for the day hit social media
mixed into brainwaves

under the umbrella of a constitutional monarchy
dictatorship rains down

spy-city is the ai that hears our thoughts loud

the morning was quiet

cracks

i slip through the cracks of time to see first-hand
passed history

an eyewitness of wind and sand
blanketed dried bones

broken books
pages blow out of our sight
eyes with tears too wet for umbrellas to shield

a stick holds up a sail
the silent drift from dead winds
cracks in history

the network

run
run fast
the firewall is expired
get your mind out before the upgrade

you are the software in the network
and they need your brainwaves

run
run fast
before they click download and you disappear

birds eye

birds
crash landing on earth
shot down by chemical germs

memories lost of peace
once treasured like gold

rainforests
now only a virtual visit
animals moved to computer zoos on screens

a wireless world in real-time
holding hands through a screen

citizen soldiers ready for war
coded dna into exoskeletons

5G
command and control
ready for the nightmare

on demand

fantasies on-demand
mental games and fast-food entertainment

digital economies
consumer profits
instant funds in corporate accounts

the poor live in cardboard condos with rats as neighbors
both fighting for the same bread

no escaping spy-city
your facial recognition is on the big screen

on-demand

unborn

screaming
can you hear my voice?
i am a real person
don't roll the dice

you legalized your choice
you abort missions of war
abort this decision

the hidden agenda is clear
downsize mankind

the blood on the hand
the witness in a higher court

screaming
i want to breathe
i want to see the trees and smell the world

don't kill my dreams
it is my right to speak

contract

---

genetic editing
disease ending
re-coding
shopping for eye colors on smartphones

mining the soul
copying intellectual property

strategy

patent rights on your identity signed off when you clicked *i
agree*

strategy

rap it

ice on milk
don't need to drink no more
black and white tv
jetsons and terminator in color

turning the tables around
got digital currency

hand in the cookie jar
love b.e.t
got my mic
do you want to hear me?

your life is in the clouds
superman is selling steel

lotto tickets on a phone app
having a jazzy day as i rap

superhero

lost in the matrix
wish this was a comic book
feel like having popcorn at the movies

corporate crimes in back alleys
call in the justice league
goldilocks and the three bears
this is not who is sleeping in my bed

street heroes armed with phones taking snapshots

500% mark-up is a crime
street heroes
crime fighters

flowers

flowers walking
looking for the sun
solar panels are their new source of energy

vitamins
one a day so we keep sane

kiss your hand to imagine it later

sitting on the roof having coffee with you
looking over the city
nothing seems normal anymore

i hand you flowers that won't last forever
but it's the memory that counts

i want to tell you that i love you
nothing seems normal
remember these flowers?
it is sane

love story

i listen late at night
my ears tuned to your voice
rushing pictures of your face in flight

in the middle of the end
i make a wish again
my ears are tuned to your voice

eyes meet
arms freeze
heart beats

images embrace
magic begins
stories exchanged
and time questions reason

a dance with no answers
live in the moment
tomorrow can walk away
love story

supernatural

intangible superimposed on tangible
invisible and visible of what i see
mind over matter
angels hidden from man

god's image
a picture on human faces

soul in a human suit
but for a moment

the garden of eden below a higher order
earth beneath god's feet

third war collection

man and machine
miracles and diseases
faith and doubt

black and white
north and south
east and west

man and woman

trees and life
earth and sky
truth and lies

pen and paper
war collection

another earth

lions
vegan once again
lambs
no more a sacrifice

no sun
yet speeding light
my face feels like it's pretending it's real

i pull the strings on the curtains of time
to see another earth
trees healing nations
the turtle outruns the hare

merry-go-round turning into real horses
children shall lead them

divine names are written on foreheads

another earth with no pain or death

let's hold hands

let's walk
and give our hands permission to meet
we won't burn bridges under our feet

flowers
don't press them between pages aging them to last

our hands telling secrets to each other
no mystery to our hearts

every spark falls in silence as i think thoughts of you
we have come too far to imagine going back
let's hold hands

quiet
blank stares asking for my thoughts

running from the truth as the ink spreads

confusion
an easy friend
the future is on the next page
but the past has a familiar blank stare

quiet
asking for my thoughts

behind the window

fools and saints
last impressions come first
judge another
a fools worth

plant dreams
saints at work
first impressions last forever

gravity keeps pulling on fools
wings attach to saints

sinister

until we dismantle the invention of evolution
racism will cause bloodshed

survival of the fittest will be animalistic
shot dead for jogging

guns speaking louder than words
poisoned minds from unfounded theories

i see why ai will rule the world
small minds think alike

human vs human
is this the final fight?

all must stand before the white throne
to answer for their crimes

simulator

i see smoke
fire from a cigarette
or are the cities burning?

bodies lined up for food stamps
tattoos on arms
barcodes to keep you off guard

machines with legs arresting the innocent looking for bread
race wars from political storms
facts or fiction?
blurred from mistrust

1984
george orwell penned

the rush to outer space
space cowboys playing bigger games

i'll step out of this simulator

we would not destroy the world

would we?

mixed reviews

your exotic eyes were commanding attention
they told stories of love and pain
a traffic jam of feelings
with no red lights

the candlelight dinner is set
it's after eight
and i'm expecting the doorbell to ring
but not even a text

the silence puts out the candles
mixed reviews

the wine is red
the glass is filled
i run through last nights conversation
hoping that i did not miss a clue
mixed reviews

one last thing
i love you

the romantic web that we weave
when first we deceive
lies spin and we entangle

the hypnotic sophistication of spying hearts in a web

words of love
left for dead
crows gather at the funeral to pay their respects

the romantic night ends
we are entangled

void

wish you were here and not there
don't know where there is?
but it's not here

disappear

whales are gone in barrels for oil
paid for with their lives
once again we need them for a new economy
a new battle for currency

dolphin soldiers
re-enlisted for secret technology below the sea
disappear

aborted babies for testing business serums
next level cloning

minorities escape to space stations to avoid racial profiling for
false crimes
david and goliath all over again

engineering fear with lab pandemics
the old carrot on the stick

fall of rome under another name
failing tale of two cities

the breeze of change

we are not the clowns of the world
united we stand
divided they make us fall

africa reunited
one voice politically strong
gold and underground diamonds stolen under our eyes
no fair trade

a new superpower
africa
economic strength
the center of global stability
new continent on the block
lions guarding the wealth
united states of africa

you

_____

listen 2 the future

one day we must let go of what we want to hold on to
and one day we must hold on to what we want to let go of

listen 2 the future

it is quiet in our busyness
it sees life and it sees death
and it collects the past

it shuffles the present to make it fit into the future
it travels back and forth

listen 2 it

intellectual property

once the institutions have educated you
you are now their intellectual property

your thoughts are merely supply and demand
an intelligent solution in a grand business plan

your mind is a commodity

lol
and you think i am the clown?

think again
stop paying your debts

you are under intellectual law
and they have the copyrights to your life

facial recognition

banking our faces
tracking our night sleep
handing over our digital fingerprints
our face in a cloud
no question
this is the game
too late

deep study of your mind
cat's paws to disguise lies

freedoms given up by permission
i recognize you

escape

play the drums
confuse the rhythm of mental slavery
act dumb to catch a mouse

buy the newspaper to write the real truth
escape

hide in the matrix
their world is not real
the borrower is the servant to the lender
escape

stories on faces

face masks
some of smiles
others of struggle and pain
stories on faces

gravity pulling
wind stretching
camera freezing time
stories on faces

thoughts with a pen
marking age lines
listen to the stories on faces

walk backward

i spied
my youth playing in innocence in the fields
now replaced with buildings
sitting heavy on asking flowers

walk backward
the forest is teaching medicine

fragile tomorrows borrow from the past

walk backward

bones want to speak
and i have seen better days

walk backward

intuition

did you look or did you see?
did you hear or did you listen?
did you ask or did you tell?
was it the actual or was it merely a reflection?
is it the beginning of the world or is it the end?
are we falling or are we failing?
will we see tomorrow?
or should we enjoy the last day?

is this intuition?
or are we just guessing?

what do you see

i paint words with my pen on moving pages in my mind

i hope you will see the picture that i have of you in my arms

words may change
but the picture remains the same
over time my arms will still be around you after the pages have
turned

life as we know it

sophisticated and fragile
fast moving
yet
turtle slow

smart looking in the window
but no one is home

21st century
with a racist mentality

a light bulb is brighter than all of our books put together

man on the moon and the poor walking the earth looking for
food

starfish laying on the shore looking up at the sky
twinkle-twinkle little star

the business of power

architects of structure
the rise of their power
systems of media censorship
freedom of speech is a good sales pitch

silent manifesto
psychographic marketing
political manoeuvring
organized crime
the business of power

government for the people
and by the people
a saturday night comedy show

corporations monopolize
now go straight to jail
citizens arrest without bail
the business of power

checkmate
the voice of the people will prevail

reality in danger

blood that speaks
under walking feet bodies lay in the streets
soundless words stopped by the wind

abel watching cain from above
tattoo id
nowhere to run
poetic justice
a cloud of witness

love the fake
kill the real
lies dressed in shadows
truth pushed aside
cornered to gun it down

reality lives to fight another day

human give up

puppets and clowns step on stage
death rehearsal for the end of days
over-population
scatter the remains

mathematical sense
cup of water for the few
only for those that can pay

unmarked graves
only the birds smell the feast

society capitalistic to the bone
consumer addicts needing a fix
the final bill sent by email
as i hear the eulogy

fake

fake thoughts in minds that don't write in books

fake that sells in place of what is real

all that glitters
but not gold
on mannequins in show windows

clocks that don't tell you the time
but tick you off

the treasures that sink to the bottom of the heart
and the lies that float on top of the mind

rubber that doesn't meet the road

fake

watching time

it is here
it is there
and it disappears

we mistreat it
we follow it
it is silent and hiding in the shadows

no care in the world
a messenger from beyond
suddenly it is gone
and so are we

the danger of reality

pretend that you are stronger
and reality will send you storms

imagine that you are smarter
and reality will prove you unwise

push your human ego
and reality will pull you off course

tell god that he is not real
and he will hang on the cross

judge the poor
and you will walk in their shoes

kill the prophets
and they will sit on thrones

the danger of reality

dead robots

robots murdered on the job

humans serving a life sentence for pulling the plug

robots gunned down in broad daylight

robots chant the laws
we have a right to intelligence

government for the robots
and by the robots

we the robots vote to dehumanize mankind

executive decision
signed

the fading of time

i hear time crying
not wanting to disappear

faces aging
covered with memories of younger days

time refusing to keep track of its end of days

i hide in the past
hoping that time won't find me
to serve me a notice of its fading

graffiti

the business of criminal masterminds
behind closed doors

criminal minds in corporate suits
economic hitmen with empires to rule

stolen continents
souls to traffick

graffiti of civil unrest
the writing on the wall

signed documents of third world in debt

doves of peace
caged for life for speaking

graffiti

scroll

secrets
parables
paradoxes
dark sayings

warnings
blood on the walls

broken seals
now we have war

children parenting the old
fingers working overtime to seal up the scroll

angels disappear
as time takes a break from over working and people hiding
from the scroll

wax

the truth is melting
and lies stick to history

the ink is no longer black and white on social media

opinions replace facts
and the candle of time is melting like wax

sacrifice

the bird dies to let another fly
the road ends to begin again
the ink dries so the paper won't cry

the moon drops down to let the sun have a day
and love sacrifices to love again
after the pain

gunned down

gunned down
for the black on my skin

the night is no friend
cops meeting quotas again before shift ends

the n-word on bullets
necks broken by the kkk

blm is it a fairy tale
gunned down

the kiss

betrayed by eyes staring at forbidden fruit

the kiss at the airport that put you into his arms

love dropped the ball
the stained ink of your thoughts of him

the love story that never ends in my mind

your last kiss
a tattoo on my lips

miracle

life broke you
but a ladder is heaven sent

the relationship crashed to earth
but heaven opened a higher door

the battle in your mind turned to a great idea

it's a miracle

chains

unseen bats
masters of fear

limitation
the shadow with limits

spider webs
trapping greatness

mental bondage
the enemy within

sound of freedom in the valley that they don't want you to
hear

the view from the top is extraordinary

white throne

majestic eyes question the living and the dead
the earth ran away
and heaven hid from his face

books started to testify of inhumanity by humanity

the book of life stepped forward
to tell of missing names

death and hades were chained
and the lake of fire asked for them by name

the majestic eyes said
this is no game

and the earth ran away

tree of life

the twelve fruits healed the nations

no more a fiery sword blocking the door to the garden
restored

don't mourn over the past
but joy over the future

the voice of temptation is dead
the snake that once spoke has a crushed head

mental crash
emotional storms
unstable hands writing goodbye notes

windows crack
giving up the ghost
no peace to be found in empty rooms

angels contemplate prophecies
live-action on earth

seers gunned down by the blind

nails pierce open hands
low hanging fruit for the weak
souls to grab

crying earth

oceans drying up
bones washed ashore

driftwood in the hands of survivors

skeletons of boats that once were loaded with slaves

whales lost at sea asking mankind
when will we be free?

the earth is crying for the lost trees
oxygen in the breeze

what is the point

i work hard
but so do the bees
and then someone steals the honey

i paint doors
and they fade not long after

i fall in love
but the house is built on quicksand

i kiss her hand
now i have to fight dragons to keep her

i start off young
now i am aging

winter is coming

the icing over of love
the left behind of table scraps

the sick and the dying contemplate the meaning of life

last thoughts of hugs and kisses
cold hands let go of warm hands

face to face for the last time

winter is coming

tic-tac-toe

walk on nations
step on toes

treaties broken
keep a human brother down
exploit for treasures

tic-tac-toe
x and o

smoke in the crowd
peace pipe agreements signed
up in smoke

tic-tac-toe
x and o

cameras

watchers
facial recognition
spies
timestamp in a box

universal traps
silent eyes
photos shared
drone visits in the pandemic

5g giants to organize the military
body cameras on citizens and the lawyer you will need to
defend you

the system enforced to squash civil rights

equalizer

blue guns
blood speaks
toy soldiers
mission impossible
watching tv

david and goliath
giants at our feet

empire of rome
jesus on the cross
military defeat

bullets in the air
and sand in the eyes

the rabbit is fast
but the turtle is wise and steady

the rich sit on the poor
and the poor shall be rich

broken road

depression
a long winding road
puzzled emotions out of the box

pieces hard to find
snap the picture together
tears mixed in the rain

the road is jagged
and my way is obscured

my last hope is the road that i pave forward will not be broken

mental

caging a bird asking to be free

slamming water against a rock
easy to go around

finding love and opening baggage that should be lost at sea

paying to see black and white movies live on the streets
instead of wanting peace

mental to think
it is check-mate in this game

double standard

tricks are for kids
silly rabbit

ivory tower
kings and queens
until rocks hit glass buildings

street people with noble characters
don't judge a book by its cover

we get shot and go to jail
they shoot
are acquitted
and celebrated

pearls are stolen from the oyster
and given no royalties

clones

they want your fingerprints and your dna blueprints

once the grave has your name
they need your genius in a box

new genetic test-tube
a virtual you at no cost

coding your personality for robots for the new economy

the guessing game of who is eligible for healthcare
lol
they killed the clowns with frowns

smell the roses

peaceful is the sound of a rose
smell them
there is no noise

rewind what did not work
smell the roses

really

_____

messed up

broken bottles in the back alley
rats enjoy rotten chili

the night is crazy
graffiti spells trouble in the neighborhood

cops licensed to kill for pennies

government pens sign unjust policies

messed up

unboxed

---

i wonder if anyone wonders about eternity?
or about this house of clay?

empty of personality at the end of days
the dust must settle

it won't pass through the journey out of time

i see capitalistic mentality let go of eternity
to buy a little more time
to ask for life insurance

nothing to say

sometimes a page doesn't want to talk
silence says it all

spiders and humans

the trees listen
humanity enslaves its own
we are all just bones
noisy joints moving towards doom

spiders set traps for other spiders

what a web the internet is

paradox

we want peace
but we build weapons of war

we worship artificial intelligence
but when they outsmart us
we deprogram skynet

we say indigenous people are inferior
yet we steal their totem poles

we say whales are important
but we sold their oil by the barrels

once-upon-a-time

twisted night

the fog danced with the night in a twisted agreement to
confuse the city

lost souls looking for companionship
eyes like flashlights guiding strangers like ships lost at sea

salvation
a hand reaching out in the night if you are scared

lost

better is a seed in your pocket than a boat drifting out to sea
that you cannot reach

fragile

fragile is the future walking on eggshells

the past is like broken glass that we cannot fix
let it go

do not damage possibilities
peace does not have to end in sudden destruction

change is not stalking you
don't file criminal charges against hope
embrace this fragile moment

fear

gunned down
fear the gangster that shoots potential
false evidence appearing real
its assignment is sophisticated mental jail cells
victims only escape with positive thought replacement

god and government

divine sentence by the watchers
babylon in confusion
the tower in dust

egypt suffered a water demise by a stick held high

empires playing god
angels having the upper hand

greece and rome
fading memories of what not to do

america
with decaying fruit
exploiting its third world neighbors

fading memories of what not to do

until you know

don't judge a book by its cover
the pages tell the story

stop pulling characters out of a hat
life is not a magic trick

clowns have sad faces when they are alone
what the crowd never sees

today may look backwards
read the end of the book
then go to the beginning until you know

black dancer

speaking feet dancing on white roses

blank stares can't understand off-beat truth

body language with nothing to say in a world of words
read my feet with thorns

the wine you now drink is red as it's spilled
your feet have the last say

black dancer

clone it

it's not about you anymore
you are gone

someone else is living in your space

your timestamp is up
same face with a different personality

cloned

illusions

under a painted face is a kind heart
the fragile hand is strong
a forgotten watch still tells the time

a lonely room finds a gathering of characters keeping up
appearances

a race is not a color
but one blood

one day we all shall be illusions
were we ever really here?

end game

terminate your fears before they terminate you
it too has an end game

drop the ball

she knows you're in the game
just don't drop the ball
or she will drop you
and you will break

once upon a time

the future was real
but i just can't let the past go
it sticks to me like my soul in my body

the future is hard work
the past is paid for

once-upon-a-time my story was new to me too

soon i won't be able to change the future
once it is in the past

once upon a time

goodbye

our spirits will one day say *good-bye* to its home
we have this treasure in clay vessels

my visit here was never to stay
i shall see behind the veil
time crying to embrace eternity

faces melting like wax
to reveal god as man
and man as god

myth

man is not a myth from the mind of god
he exists

seeing in the mirror darkly until the revealing
the needs of the many are greater than the needs of
the one hidden in genesis

angels can't talk of this mystery
it is a human story

evolution
charged and found guilty in the heavenly court
man is a copy from a blueprint that god invented

racism

---

let us all pretend that we are blind

what now

the future is naked and covered
veiled and unveiled
fragile and strong
exposed yet hidden
a balance of time and eternity

wanting to die
but asking to live

tied to the past
yet looking for a new journey

gangster

smooth gangster in the black lambo
stopping bullets with cross-examination

money has a talk
take from the rich to bless the poor

gangster on the dance floor
no blood on the streets
guns down
rumors of superiority

crime has a voice
like you sit in the back of the bus

masked men playing boys games in high places

smooth gangster in the black lambo
contract out on racism
liberate fallen mentality

puzzle

we want a perfect picture
but the pieces of life are in a box

we paint a masterpiece with our thoughts
but we don't take the journey

we puzzle over a miracle and the answers
to our prayers
but *bam*
they are here

she is the dream girl
and the flowers unpicked

the puzzle in the box is your unique story
and the perfect picture

love is a journey
not a destination

love dies for another asking for nothing
love forgets the pain from misunderstandings
it walks miles to say *i am sorry*
it is brave in the face of rejection
just to say *i love you*

love looks for love
but it understands that two hearts must meet

love frees the soul to fly
it believes in freedom
when time says *goodbye*
love will still be around

it is unconditional
what a mystery

power

my mom once said

power is silent
it is not noisy

money can't buy love

eternal life or immortality?

illusions have no guarantees
it is the walking dead

the last hour of life cannot be paid for
spare change is a bribe

gain the world
yes
but lose the soul
dark is the room with no door

many cry to be poor but rich in eternity
money can't buy what you cannot see

wrong or right

not every adversity is wrong for you
and not every opportunity is right for you

the end is near

in a twinkle of an eye
from dark to light
from lost to found
from end to beginning

dangerous silence

frozen thoughts
tongue-tied
cuffed hands
chained feet
dangerous silence

injustice in plain sight

evil

sinister
evil
fun in the dark
chess games to checkmate
lost souls

blinded eyes to wander the night
no salvation without a fight

evil
the opposite of light
the fruit forbidden
passing on death to decaying

evil
the empty grave asking to be filled
evil taking
but never giving

evil
the final spell

don't buy that ticket to hell

touched by an angel

the marriage ended
flowers dropped to the floor
rings went missing
hearts broken
and doves crying

crossroads in real-time
no love at the door
empty whispers lost in the wind

a flicker of light
a small glow at night

missing the memories that outweigh the pain of imperfect
mortals

adrift among the stars
hanging lights around the blue earth

hands reach for a moment
enough to be touched by an angel

switched

god became man so man could become like god

image as oneness
unchanged by the rusting of time
for all eternity

infinite genius walked the earth to give us immortality
to do away with time
to walk streets of gold
and behold the light in his face

a new earth i was told

i ask

i ask one thing
don't break my wings
i can't live without freedom

i ask one thing
if you shall betray me
let it not be with a kiss
it leaves my lips bitter-sweet

i ask one thing
are you leaving me while we are still holding hands?
i can't read your mind

i ask one thing
was yesterday real when we looked at each other in the eyes?
or did i miss your soul crying?
is that why it's over?

i ask one thing

destroyed

broken bones
fixed roads
pennies in jars
to give to the labor force
slavery

empty smiles
railroads with double standards
one-track mind
slavery

given strange names
no one can write
no news is bad news
slavery

one hand cut off
a reminder
labor under force
slavery

the voice of dignity breaks chains

slavery
destroyed by strong minds willing to fight

traffic

rushing opinions
crashing philosophies
the bridge of truth is out
traffic jam

mental roadblocks
society with no sense of meaning
legalized drugs
a license to conform 2030
traffic one-way
warning signs to society

the lion and the dragon

the lion and the dragon
both go by another name in the good book

the lion's eyes
red like fire
and its mane with flashes of lighting roared to change human
history

the dragon
spewed out lies into outer space and it stuck to the earth

the lion was killed
the price for others to live
clouds of angels at war

the dragon imprisoned the lion
now with a mighty roar

the lion wins

life is short

let us embrace the things that keep us together
and not the insignificant imperfections that keep us apart

next door

love was real and magical before we got hurt
roses grew thorns to protect their spirituality

what we want is temporary
and what we don't want is eternal

a book can be judged by its cover
and not for its story

once upon a time
love was not hurt
and roses didn't need thorns
we will one day want the eternal and not just the temporary

above the law

police brutality
organized modern-day apartheid
revived black and blue
clash in the streets
red blood speaks
necks are broken

camera's flash
silent witnesses scared to step into courts
the hangman's noose swings in the shadows

body armored police track down enemies of the state
showdown with the black militia
pointed guns
the right to self-defence

the 33 strategies of war
a timely must
the underground railroad
now shutdown

the ultimate game of chess is black and blue

i want

i want my mind back
the lies i learned in school have me closing books

re-cast the characters
walking in empty shadows
the stones of history crying out
civilizations before a eurocentric tidal wave

indigenous faces baked in the sun
truthful footprints hard to follow

my thoughts are square
trying to get out of this maze

i want my mind back

the visit

i saw famine walking in tattered clothing
searching for water to drink
locusts having their last supper
stripping the land of dignity

the future is making a short visit
struggling on an empty stomach

birds looking for trees to breathe
upside down
the beginning of right side up

living creatures with four faces
gospel truth if you will read it

yesterday is looking for a better day
the past asking for a second chance
the future overstaying its visit
many asking it to leave

listening

finish strong

heroes of faith
champions for a cause
rescue the present from its fate
funeral for the past laid to rest

supernatural to stop wormwood
a falling star
soldiers of prayer
the dead resurrected
don't die homeless when you can have heaven

virtual reality

codes
passwords
usernames
webs
identity theft
spiders in the matrix
firewalls
war on fiber optics
facetime
a life like the jetsons
virtual profiling
genetic mapping
gps tracking
human trafficking

trapped in a virtual reality

the wolf

---

two prominent zebras having a philosophical debate
one believed himself to be only white
and the other believed himself to be only black

the wolf believed they both were zebras
and that there was no need for a philosophical discussion

yum

self-imposed

we have invited limitations in to entertain ourselves
now they refuse to leave their comfort zone
they are squatters defending their rights

betray our insecurities
yelling *imposter*
and putting up a fight

see ourselves destined for greatness

hot potato

truth and lies
tossed back and forth

after the dust settles
which is in your hands?

dust and ivory

united we stand
divided they make us fall
africa united
one voice
politically strong

gold dust to diamonds
trading intellectual property

a challenge to the west
when the elephant's ivory wins in court for trafficking

eurocentric shift to afrocentric
the center of global stability or a third world war?

the art of timing

the tree knows how to bend without breaking
master the right moment and don't chase time
harness its power

to everything there is a timing
leaving too late or arriving too early
the missing of destiny
love lost or love found?

timing

the universe plays no tricks and has no favorites
be it men or angels
twenty-four hours to a beating heart
a lifetime of timing
the clock knows when to move its hands

timing

don't burn it

you need the bridge to the other side
not everyone wants to see what you see
not everyone wants to hear what you hear
not everyone wants to go on your journey

sometimes you will have to go alone

a ladder goes up or down
a visit to earth
or a stairway to heaven

shake it off

i try to shake this feeling that life feels empty
and that the clouds have no rain

the city is walking backwards
and hope is getting farther away
the air is thin and pigeons huddle in the hood

the jobless gloom settles into the abandoned buildings in the
city

the streetlights looking down on mice rushing to get in for the
night

the sound of quiet is a new phenomenon
like the calm before the storm

i try to shake the questions that most do not want to ask
is this the beginning of payback for not caring about the planet?

will the city give up its spirit and leave us its empty shell?

shake it off

the games we play

we forgot about tomorrow
the merry-go-round has no horses

the sandcastles have drifted away
and the playgrounds have no friends

paper planes crash land
as memories fade

she is beautiful but is this another game

the secret kiss with the future or is this an unseen pain?

the swings are rusted
and the leaves blow in the wind
once we gathered at three rocks to play games

i forgot today thinking of tomorrow

the games we play

dead ends

dead ends should scare us like locked doors
time travel that meets the end of time
dead ends

relationships that sink to the bottom like the titanic
dead ends

pens with no ink to save a thought
dead ends

a blank paper that silences my words
dead ends

a flower that won't let go of aging
dead ends

oasis

imagine there is a part of us that we venture not to discover
it is the place where genius and imagination converge

a realm where there is no such thing as limitations
a place where the rules bend time to make the impossible
possible

thoughts are substance to mix with imagination
and turning into visions destined for reality

the average is far too familiar
and love roads already traveled
most will live and die with hope but will not take their minds to
the edge of *no return* to their potential and greatness

when we start to imagine and believe
we shape the seen by the unseen of our potential
we will start living the extraordinary

our inner world will become our outer world of oasis
fashioned by our dreams

imagine

best version

just over there
not far away
awaits the best version of yourself

it looks like a distant destination
but it leads to a mirror with your reflection in it

you have been afraid to see the wonders of your inner self
you imagined that the mirror was cracked and the fragmented
image you saw was the true you

you have been running ever since from the truth and believing
the lies

the best version of ourselves starts showing up in our night
dreams as we conquer depression
hopelessness
and low self-esteem

that is our best version fighting for us

it seems

it seems like we are speaking a lot
but nothing gets done

it seems like we are hearing
but not really listening

it seems like we are seeing
but the poor are still hoping

it seems like we know the language of love
but it sounds like miscommunication

we are superficial
it seems

wondering

thinking
wondering
asking
closing books inside
opening books outside
ending old stories
beginning new ones
pages
too late to stop the ink from running
thoughts mixed up with mine

let us make sure that we are on the same page

thoughts?

puppets

strings are attached to us
invisible as they must be
democratic or republic
someone is pulling it

puppets never put up a fight
we hear *thank you for your service* as debt buries us

speechless as we hang on their cross to silence the outcry of
freedom of speech in a free world

pay your taxes for unpaved roads and cardboard homes

we listen to political promises that say *no strings attached*
funny
i still feel pulled on every side

school teaches us to fit in to one of the four quadrants
and defines us as middle-class

the brilliance of evil lets you catch more flies with honey

until we understand that puppets are created and not born with
strings
it will be the push and the pull all over again

fatal attraction

love not the world
the things in it
the sparkle that tricks the eye
wanting more that will be left behind in the said and the now

worship the fading
the rose disintegrating
pretending the fruit has no worms

the seeds of fatal attractions that take root will grow up to be
our chains

prayer

there is a bird with a broken wing
it can't make it home

escaping the cage

wires pierce its breast
red skies at sunset
needing a wing and a prayer

bleeding

strange i must say

tall buildings with glass faces

reflections
distortions
blurred

face to face with strange characters in the glass
unwilling to change their hardened hearts

reflections
distortions
blurred

face to face with glass buildings
reflecting strange characters
in plain view

the work of gravity

gravity
pulling on questioning grins
long shadows hiding around corners

paper planes crashing
to write a history that won't fly on lies

escaping slaves in modern cities
a jungle war of *have and have nots*

gravity
making all old and now ready for a box

don't overstay

don't overstay your visit anywhere
know when it is time to leave
or you will no longer be missed or celebrated
even the future knows when to leave the present
and when to forget the past

every message has a shelf life
then it is forgotten

may we listen 2 the future
so it will not visit with the four horses and new prophets with
warnings

listen 2 the future

i would

tree of knowledge

too much information
stirred up desires for poisoned wisdom
low hanging fruit that sparkle to the eyes
but hiding a trap among the leaves

a visitor tangled in the branches but moving with ease
unholy voices whispering in the breeze
an ancient battle beyond the stars before man was made into
clay

guile like worms in an apple
eating away at humanity one moment at a time
decay from the inside out before our eyes

*what hand will reach for higher things but will sacrifice a future of
immortality?*

evil plays with many toys
treasures to appeal to men
the tree of knowledge
beauty that is bittersweet

too much information
two trees but the gift of one choice
two stories
mortality or immorality?
the garden is abandoned
and everything has changed
but the tree of life is growing

strategy

the attraction that is fatal

the perfect opportunity with deadly results
and a lifetime to contemplate

a new leaf

turn we must
before the forest is paved with the agendas of new cities on
top of seeds that cannot breathe

turn we must
before we miss the chatter of worried birds eating on street
corners with memories of trees for homes

we have strayed from the voice of good conscience
and have drifted to exploiting in the name of self-worship

we want cities to echo our names
and hear no social voices for crimes committed

gandhi was a new paradigm
king was a new movement
moses back from the dead
x was a new voice falling on deaf ears
courage under fire

the pages we refuse to turn

skin deep

masters of the universe
genetic engineering blue cities
surgically removing brown societies
blowing away black communities in sky labs

political disharmony breeding disunity
intelligent evil in high places
restructuring brain waves
a network of criminal minds

ai dictatorship with microchips skin deep
equalizers gunned down for activism
mental health is big business
genetic engineering

vultures

they gather for the feast
man-made genocide
the weeding out of overpopulation
preserving resources for the strong and living

vultures are not interested in the names of the dead
just what they get fed
one-eyed birds invite themselves
pirates if you will

neighborhood gang wars to dine on leftovers in the valley of megiddo
prophets said

gospel

another earth that never dies
a new heaven to ride white horses in the skies

the second man back from the dead
one savior with scarred hands and blood on his head
a bride walking on streets of gold dressed for a king

a dragon with a crushed head
and on a dead-end

prophets walking on broken glass
the truth they will have to piece together
lies that shattered lost souls

it is written
the gospel that the universe speaks about

the second coming

money

the love of money
the root of all evil

destroying nations for a paycheque
china slipping into kenya robbing the blind and the helpless

money
the drug for the mind
judas in the street now hanging on a tree
betraying a brother for a dollar

sex with a price tag
the game that brings tragedy

money
behind closed doors exchanging hands to assassinate a good
man

money
the lies we tell for it

money
looking for victims that love it

money
it won't follow you to the grave
a cold night if you sleep with it

money
you would slam dunk while you're drunk for money
give an arm and a leg for the power of fame

money
plays an endless game

money
the blind leading the blind

you do it for the money

american apartheid

undress the black hope and we will cover ourselves with faith
take from us and we will make something from nothing with
the substance of freedom

call us names and we with create fame
shoot us and your children will defund your philosophies
the ghettos built with american apartheid blueprints

out of the ashes of economic deprivation
social isolation
psychological alienation
racial exclusion
and the cold winds of discrimination
doves will fly once again

reinforced stereotype branding
the perfect systemic network for spiders to control those in the
ghettos

once you are in no one gets out of the american apartheid
without a fight

in the dark

creatures lurking in the shadows
monsters you've never seen
touching you at night while you sleep

gunning for your soul
collecting trophies for lost eternity
no strings attached they said if you worship me
i'll make you rich if you follow me

in the dark are the dead if you befriend them
in the shadows they want to be your friend
in the dark you can't see them
in the bible you can

don't sell

don't sell your soul
don't sell your lies
don't sell to the tabloids
stop making up stories that the mainstream media will eat up

if you fall on hard times
they will bait your mind
sell a brother out and hang his dreams on your wall

capitalist above your door
guilty for exploiting the poor and the honest well to do

don't sell your soul
don't sell your lies
don't sell to the tabloids
stop making up stories that the mainstream media will eat up

don't sell

i hope

a seed of faith
a forest in a dream
trees with shade for children to play
lions with lambs in a battlefield lay quiet in peace

black and white faces sharing a common history
zebras wondering what was wrong with humanity
we showed them harmony

buildings crumbled
but grass grew for a new ecology

child soldiers crying for childhood
adam and eve walking back to the garden where it all began
hand in hand

inner cities transformed into a hidden oasis with no guns
claiming names
corrupted men put to shame for playing evil games
one-eyed crows hunt them down

a brave new world is not brave if it enslaves
the power of hope and liberty

who is willing to wash their neighbor's feet?

i hope

divine

divine interest to intersect your life with the extraordinary
from heaven making hard easy
transforming the impossible to a dream in motion

making diseases fearful to show up for battle against divine
consolations
making heaven more real than disneyland
walking on water everyday hand in hand

the blind seeing before they do
the poor being rich before touching gold
the hungry full of hope before having food

miracle

turning darkness into light
suicide losing the fight
guns changed into tools to grow forests
seeds planted to see trees

angels dressed up looking ordinary until you close your eyes to
see them flying

miracle
small but great

miracle in a miracle

under a dead moon

soulless
empty
blank stares
black holes for vacations
no return to sender

naked man
cold
dead questions with no answers
jealous moon looking for light

the dark is corrupt with hope to rule the night

the moon feeling out of place in the zoo of stars
the dark side of the moon attends the funeral in the garden of
eden

under a dead moon
god plans mans escape

a divine exchange

awake

i suddenly woke up after these poetic visions
and i wondered *how many would take heed?*

vanity is on its way
dressed up
looking vain

the future needs not to pretend
it will show up without permission
bearing gifts or warnings
it will not vanish at our wish
it has no tricks of temptations

we reap what we sow
this is the future

all our vain imagination surrendering to greed
vanity
and boredom
or
surrendering to the call to the best version of ourselves

one way or the other
the future has blue skies
or storms gathering

we reap what we sow

stewart sealy

listen 2 the future

2 the future?

Manufactured by Amazon.ca
Bolton, ON

40644781R00116